Biodynamics for the home Garden

Peter Proctor

D1603040

© 2011 Peter Proctor / Cloud South Films Ltd.

All Rights Reserved. Please note you do not have
any giveaway rights or resale rights to this ebook.
Thank You.

Published in New Zealand by Sumner Burstyn
F / 19 Blake Street Ponsonby, Auckland 1011
www.cloudsouth.co.nz
Publication Date: 5/2011

ISBN 978-0-473-188337   (e-book)

Cover design by Ruth Mitchener, 2011

Front Garden

CONTENTS

CONTENTS

CONTENTS

PREFACE

The home garden in a busy urban environment can be a quiet space where it is a joy to walk around after a busy working day. A nicely laid out garden with a balance of flowers, vegetables, fruit and berry trees, flowering shrubs set out in reasonably tidy lawns can be a joy to the soul.

There is a lovely feeling in a garden, which after a stressful working day can be a healing balm. What is it that makes these vegetables grow so well? How is it that the flowers in their season treat these gardeners to waves of colour and scents? I think it is because they love their garden and the garden loves them.

As they stroll around, the gardeners have the opportunity to pick and eat a handful of raspberries or blackberries growing on the fence, or gather them for the evening dessert. They may even pick up a large juicy feijoa or two to eat as they walk; maybe even to munch on that newly ripened tomato or chew on that soft tasty sweet corn. And then to walk over the soft springy lawn with that sweet scent that can only come from the freshly mown grass completes this pleasant garden experience.

Time to look at that compost heap that was made during the weekend…..is it heating up properly, is the smell telling us the compost is breaking down in the right way?

Then, oh joy, a chance to rest awhile on the garden seat under the big apple tree, for a welcome cup of tea, and ponder "what a lovely a garden thou art ".

These gardeners enjoy their home grown vegetables and fruit because they taste so wonderful. So what shall they gather for the evening meal? It could be a salad of lettuce, cucumber, rocket, tomato, coriander and chives or perhaps a cooked meal of silver beet, broccoli, kumara, carrot, potato and onion. They never tire of these foods.

CHAPTER 1

WHAT IS BIODYNAMIC GARDENING?

Biodynamic gardening is essentially an organic system of gardening, but one that uses particular preparations made from cow dung, silica crystals and various medicinal herbs.

These preparations that are either sprinkled on the land to enhance microbial life in the soil, sprayed in a mist over the leaves of the plants to enhance photosynthesis and strengthen the plant or put into composts and liquid manures to assist the proper breakdown of the organic matter. Farmers and gardeners say that using the Biodynamic system of agriculture makes organic farming and gardening work!

Firstly, what is understood about the concepts of organic farming? Organic farming is, at its core, about the health of the soil. Before the advent of modern agricultural techniques, around the beginning of the 20th century, all agricultural soils right across the world would have been healthy and living and managed organically. This has been documented in many articles written on soil written at that time. Unfortunately modern agricultural techniques have escalated since the mid 1960s, meaning that much agricultural research and agricultural technologists have concentrated on the N P K theory of plant nutrition.

Modern agricultural science holds the belief that to feed a hungry world and meet the demand for an increase in food supply, artificial forms of Nitrogen in the form of Urea (N); Phosphorous, in the form of Super Phosphate (P) and Potash in the form of Muriate of Potash (K) and all micronutrients such as Boron, Copper, Zinc, Cobalt, Magnesium etc, must be added in some form of a chemical salt to grow food. The use of agricultural chemicals since the Second World

War has resulted in major degeneration of soils throughout the world. This chemical approach has largely destroyed the humus which had developed in the soils over the centuries in agricultural countries all over the world. This has resulted in a massive loss of soil fertility which has led plants to become increasingly susceptible to disease and insect pests; there is also a consequent loss in nutritional quality in all foods.

Because the soil has lost its humus, there is less water holding capacity, the roots do not penetrate as deeply into the soil, there is less depth of root in the plants, and because there is less water holding capacity in the soil there is a greater need to irrigate in dry weather. Together with the pollution of agricultural chemical residues in the soil seeping into ground water, the world supply of drinking water is threatened.

There is a challenge to modern agriculture to change the growing systems to something more living. The organic farmer / gardener maintains the fertility of their soil using organic materials, such as animal dung, composts, liquid manures, green manures and crop rotation. All that is stated here applies equally well to the home garden as it does to any commercial horticultural or agricultural activity.

CHAPTER 2

THE IMPORTANCE OF HUMUS IN THE GARDEN

When one digs up a piece of soil in a biodynamic garden the first thing you notice is how easily the spade goes into the soil. The second thing is how well the soil breaks up if you drop a piece from chest height to the ground.

Break open one of these pieces of soil and observe the crumbly nature. This will vary depending on the inherent nature of the soil; is it clay and heavy or is it sandy and light? In both cases there will be this crumb structure and evidence of earth worm castings and with the roots going deeply into the soil. You will notice how the soil clings to the root hairs of the plant.

Another indication of good soil structure is obvious evidence of earthworm castings in the sample and the mixing of the top soil with the subsoil. This is seen where the topsoil and subsoil meet and the earthworm castings blend the soils of different colours together.

To check the humus in your soil, take your soil profile and feel how slippery the soil is at the top of the profile when rubbed between ones finger and thumb and then note how it becomes gritty lower down in the profile. The slippery feel indicates the presence of humus and the gritty feel indicates lesser humus.

WHAT IS HUMUS?

- Humus is organic carbon which is the result of the final breakdown of organic matter. Such substance is colloidal dark brown in colour and slippery to the feel.
- Humus makes the soil more open and light.

- It allows greater water penetrability, greater water retention and encourages deep root development.
- It encourages earth worm activity.
- It encourages a strong microbiological activity, like nitrogen nodulation on the roots of legumes.

THE PART THAT HUMUS PLAYS IN HEALTHY SOIL

- Soils that have high humus content will also have the biological activity to convert plant residues, leaf litter, animal dung and various biomasses into stable humus.
- Humus gives the soil the ability to absorb and retain moisture. Such soils do not dry out and require significantly less irrigation.
- Humus provides a reservoir for the plant nutrients available in the soil for balanced plant growth.
- Humus plays a part in supporting soil bacteria such as rhizobacta, which is important for all legume nodulation and other well known bacteria such as the phosphate solubilizing bacteria.
- The exudates from bacterial activity will result in a sticky substance called polysaccharides being released which helps bind the small soil particles into a nutty crumb structure to a depth of 30cm or more.
- Humus also supports the all important mycorrhizal fungi which form a symbiotic relationship with many plants.

The thread like roots, or hyphae, from these fungi, which are one micron in diameter, attach themselves to the roots of the host plant and source nutrients and moisture from long distances in exchange for carbohydrates from the plant. These mycorrhizal fungi hyphae also bind the soil and give it a good crumb structure. This good structure makes cultivation easier and creates better tilth, enabling better seed sowing and planting.

We can see these "soil forming webs" of mycorrhizal fungi hyphae if we look in the leaf mould under trees in a forest. A singular mycorrhizal fungi can become very large and its hyphae are reported to cover the area of two sports fields. These organisms also associate to form what are now being called "food webs" to provide food or nutrition to the plant. On a farm it is said that the weight of the organisms in the soil is equal to the weight of the animals above the ground that the land can support.

The micro organisms are bacteria including rhizobia and azobacta (nitrogen fixing), phosphate solubilizing bacteria, mycorrhizal fungi and other beneficial fungi, algae, actinomycetes, and protozoa, and there are the macro organisms such as nematodes, springtails, mites, ants, millipedes and earthworms. All these micro and macro organisms are important factors in the soil food web.

A strong biological soil life encourages an active worm population. Earthworm castings have more readily available plant nutrients for the plant than the surrounding soil itself. As observed before a soil profile will feel smooth and silky where there is humus, as opposed to a rough sandy feel in silty, granity or volcanic soils and a sticky feel in clay soils. Usually the higher humus content is near the top few centimetres of the soil.

There are four ways that the home gardener can increase and then maintain humus in the soil:

1. By making and using as much Biodynamic compost as possible.
2. By growing green crops in between the growing of vegetable or flower crops.
3. Regularly applying the biodynamic cow horn preparation 500 and CPP.
4. By applying preparation 501 to make strong plants whose leaves are carbon rich and when decomposed will add to the organic carbon or in its final form humus (see Chapter 3.)

Your local Biodynamic Association will have a supply of all these biodynamic preparations available.

The Organic farmer / gardener would practise the following management techniques to maintain such a sustainable system:

- Composts. Made from animal manures which are usually combined with plant materials, such as green legume crops and dry strawy material where the organic materials are converted into stable humus through a fermentation process using the biodynamic preparations 502 to 507 (see Chapter 3).
- Liquid Manures made from animal manures, lucerne, beneficial weeds, seaweed powder or kelp.
- Making a Cow Pat Pit which cow dung fermented with the biodynamic preparations 502 to 507(see Chapter 6).
- Growing a green manure in between crops.
- Practising crop rotation.

Composting the organic materials will avoid the nutrient losses from oxidation or leaching that would occur if these materials were to be applied directly on the ground. Various rock dusts can be applied through the compost heap to supply any depleted essential mineral elements like rock phosphate.

CHAPTER 3

THE BIODYNAMIC PREPARATIONS

What does Biodynamic agriculture offer the organic gardener?

The organic gardener does everything which is more or less accepted in worldwide agricultural circles as the way of working organically. All fertility inputs will be in an organic form such as animal dung, liquid manures and composts made with a wide range of natural organic materials. The organic gardener will continue to garden as before, but experience has shown that the use of the biodynamic techniques can make all these organic processes described, work more quickly and effectively.

Biodynamics works from two poles. One pole is the importance of maintaining sustainable soil fertility in an organic way using composts, liquid manures, green cropping and mulching. Biodynamic agriculture uses a series of preparations numbered from 500 to 508 which are based on various mineral, plant, and animal substances. The use of these will enhance all the bacterial, fungal and mineral processes that are found in organic gardening systems and help to sustain the soil fertility.

The second pole is the recognition that there is a connection between plant growth and the cosmic rhythms of the sun, the Moon, the planetary movements, and their relative relationships with the Zodiac constellations. The cosmic activities can work strongly into a living soil and into the plant. This enhances the quality and life giving forces of the fruits and vegetables we eat. The working together of these two poles is what brings about healthy and nutritious plants.

Biodynamic agriculture places great importance on the relative positions of the sun, Moon and planets in relation to the Zodiac constellations when applying the biodynamic preparations, sowing seeds, planting plants, applying liquid manures or spraying fruit trees and crops (see Chapter 4 on understanding the planting calendar). The following is a brief description of the various preparations and their function:

PREPARATION 500 - COW HORN DUNG

This is known as cow horn manure, and is basically fermented cow dung. It is the basis for soil fertility, and the renewal of degraded soils. It is usually the first preparation used during the change over to the biodynamic system. It helps to develop a good soil structure and works on the root development of the plant. It works with the calcium processes in the soil. Preparation 500 is made by filling a cow's horn with cow dung, and burying it in the soil during the autumn/winter period and dug up in early spring months.

It can be sprayed up to four times a year. The best times are in spring and then again in the autumn. It is important to apply in the late afternoon during the descending period of the Moon (see chapter 4 on understanding planting calendar).

Spreading Preparation 500 with hearth brush

It is used in small quantities at the rate of 25 grams in 13 litres of water per acre. It is stirred for one hour, making a vortex or crater first in one direction and then reversing the direction and making a vortex in the other direction alternating clockwise and anti clockwise motions. Usually each movement takes approx 20 seconds the stirred preparation can then be sprinkled with a whisk brush over your garden.

With regular application, preparation 500 will give a soil all the characteristics previously discussed, such as:

• Strong humus formation.
• Increase in all soil bacteria such as an increase in nodulation on all legumes
• Increases in phosphate solubilizing bacteria.
• Increase in all beneficial soil fungi.
• Increase in the mycorrhizal fungi and their hyphae.
• Improves the crumb structure and resultant improvement in soil tilth. This means the soil can be worked easily in preparing seed beds and for planting.
• Earthworm activity is increased.
• Absorption and retention of water is greater (note that international research has found that Biodynamic soils require between 25% and 50% less irrigation than conventional soils).
• Deeper rooting system is developed in all plants.
• It will work well in any soil type.

PREPARATION 501 - COW HORN SILICA

This is fine quartz crystals ground into a powder. The crystal should be of good quality, shape and clarity. The powder is made into a slurry, put in a cow's horn in a manner similar to Preparation 500, but this time it is buried during the summer months. It works with the silica processes.

Preparation of Cow Horn Dung 500

Stirring Preparation 500 – note vortex

When lifted in autumn it is stored in glass jar on a sunny window sill. It is used mainly during the growing season and is used at the rate of 1 gram in 13 litres of water per acre. 501 is applied at sunrise as a fine mist that drifts over the plant or tree. It is used at the beginning of a plants growth and then shortly before the harvest of the plant. It is important to note that using 501 in full sunlight will cause burning to the leaves of plants.

This spray enhances the photosynthesis of the leaf, has a strengthening effect on plant growth and as such compliments the activity of the preparation 500, which works mostly in the root zone of the plant.

Preparation 501 is best sprayed when the Moon and Saturn are in opposition which occurs once each month. At this time it will strengthen the plant against fungus and insect attack (see Chapter 4 on understanding the planting calendar).

PREPARATION CLAY - COW HORN CLAY

Rudolf Steiner says that Clay and Aluminium silicate are the mediators between the processes of calcium 500 and silica 501. This prepared clay has been buried in the soil in the same way and at the same time as the horn cow dung. The

Spraying Horn Silica 501 in mist

winter horn clay is applied in the evenings at the same time as preparation 500. This is a new preparation and it is being used at the rate of 10 grams in 13 litres of water per acre. The clay preparation appears to make 500 and 501 more effective.

PREPARATIONS 502 – 507 - COMPOST

These are a series of preparations made from various medicinal herbs, in such a way as to enhance their inherent qualities. The biodynamic compost preparations 502 / 507 are applied to the compost heap when it is first made, and to any compost that is brought onto the property to aid and regulate the fermentation process. They are also used in the making of liquid manure and cow pat pit. Experience in many countries using these preparations in composts and liquid manures show us that they accelerate humus formation, and as such avoid losses of valuable plant nutrients.

Remember you can get your all your requirements of Biodynamic preparations from your local Biodynamic association. You don't have to make them yourself.

A brief description is as follows:

The Preparations 502 – 507 are made from medicinal herbs and some are made together with a particular animal part and buried in the soil much the same way as the preparation 500 is made.

502   Made from the flowers of Yarrow; Achillea millifolium
Helps processes of Potassium [K] Sulphur [S] and trace elements
Connected to planet Venus

503   Made from the flowers of German Chamomile; Matricuria chamomilla

Helps processes of Calcium [Ca] and Nitrogen [N]
Connected to planet Mercury

504   Made from the leaves and stems of Stinging Nettle; Urtica dioica
        Helps processes of Iron [Fe] and Magnesium [Mg]
        Connected to planet Mars

505   Made from the bark of the European Oak; Quercus robur
        Helps processes of Calcium [Ca]
        Connected to planet Moon

506   Made from the flowers of Dandelion; Taraxicum officinalis
        Helps processes of Silica [Si]
        Connected to planet Jupiter

507   Made from the flowers of Valerian; Valeriana officinalis
        Helps processes of Phosphorus [P]
        Connected to planet Saturn

PREPARATION 508 - EQUISETUM ARVENSE

Preparation 508 is the dried foliage of Equisetum arvense, more commonly known as Horse Tail. It is silica rich can be used as a tea to control fungus starting in the early season and continuing until harvest.

Gently boil ten grams of the dried herb in 2 litres of water for twenty minutes. Let it stand for two days. The tincture is diluted 1 to 9 and sprayed regularly onto the soil in the early spring at the rate of 40 litres per acre or 10 litres for ¼ of an acre.

The Australian She oak or Casurina stricta is commonly used around the world as a shelter and shade tree. It has high silica content in the leaf and can be used if there is a shortage of Equisetum. It is prepared in the same way as Equisetum arvense as described above or made into liquid manure.

The Equisetum 508 is best sprayed during the humid times of the Moon's cycle which is just before full Moon and at perigee (see Chapter 4 understanding the planting calendar).

A full description of how to make and how to use Cow horn dung, Cow horn silica, Cow horn clay, the making of the compost preparations 502 – 507 and how to use them in making compost, liquid manures and cow pat pit preparations is given in the book "Grasp the Nettle" How to make Biodynamic Agriculture Work, by Peter Proctor. Published Random House (2004).

SEQUENTIAL SPRAYING

Sequential spraying is when the gardener brings the influences or effects of all the preparations into the garden over a short space of time. This is usually done during a two day period. Doing so appears to make a big difference to the growth of all plants in the garden.

- Start one evening by stirring and sprinkling the ground with preparation 500 together with the cow pat pit which is made using the compost preparations 502 to 507 (see chapter 5 for the making of a cow pat pit).
- The following morning stir and spray as a mist over the plants the silica preparation 501.
- That evening the cow horn clay is stirred and sprinkled on the ground.
- Then the following morning Equisetum 508 is applied.

I like to start this sequence by applying cow horn preparation 500 and the cow pat pit on the evening before the Moon is opposite Saturn. Then 501 will be sprayed at the Moon opposite Saturn which is the right time for the strengthening of the plant.

CROP ROTATION

Planned crop rotation is an essential part of a sustainable system, particularly in market gardening or field cropping. Rotation of crops will control weeds and there will be less build up of fungus and insects. It also allows a build up of a wide range of plant nutrients and won't lead to any serious trace element deficiencies.

ESSENTIAL PLANT NUTRIENTS

Maintenance of essential plant nutrients, in particular phosphate, is important. This can be added in a natural form, as Rock Phosphate, either on a growing green crop or through a compost heap, as previously mentioned. If Calcium is needed it can be added through compost as a light dressing of hydrated lime. Agricultural lime can be used through a compost

Leeks growing well –planted in early Jan

heap if the soil is acidic.

Using cow manure and seaweed regularly through composts and liquid manures will maintain trace elements.

SUMMARY OF CHAPTER 3

- Apply preparation 500 in spring and autumn in the afternoon during a descending period of the Moon.
- Use one portion 25g of 500 in 13 litres clean unpolluted water and stirred for one hour. Sprinkle over your garden with a hearth brush. Maintains good soil structure and encourages earth worms.
- Apply preparation 501 early in the morning at sunrise near the time of the Moon opposite Saturn. Use one portion 1 gram of 501 in 13 litres of water stirred for one hour. Spray as a mist over the plants.
- Use cow horn clay as a mediator between 500 and 501. Use as part of the sequential spray. Use the compost preparations 502 to 507 in all composts, liquid manures or cow pat pits that you make. They help order the fermentation and break down of the organic matter.
- Look to using the sequential spray of all the preparations.
- Remember that you can buy the preparations that you need from your nearest Biodynamic Association.

Sweetcorn, Tomatoes, Dwarf Beans

CHAPTER 4

UNDERSTANDING THE PLANTING CALENDAR

This should be used in conjunction with the planting calendars produced by your local biodynamic association, specific to your country and hemisphere. The Moon, solar, planetary, and constellation rhythms that are considered when working with the planting and sowing calendar are described as follows:

FULL MOON

Waxing (new to full) and Waning (full to new)
Occurs approx every 29 1/2 days.

- In the 48 hours leading up to full Moon there appears a distinct increase in the moisture content of the earth. The growth forces of the plants seem to be enhanced.
- The full Moon period is connected with the growth tendency of the plant with quick germination of seeds, fast growth and a rapid re-growth of any cut, mown or pruned vegetation. There appears to be quicker cell division and tendency towards elongation of growth.
- Seed germination is fast but may be soft and prone to fungus attack, particularly in warm conditions and high humidity.
- The influence of the full Moon appears to provide favourable conditions for the growth of fungus on all plants.
- There is an increase in insect activity, particularly slugs and snails, and internal worm parasites in humans and animals.
- These conditions allow for good absorption of liquid manures.
- Often there is a tendency for rain at full Moon.

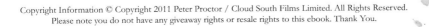

ACTIVITIES CONNECTED WITH FULL MOON

- Sow seeds at times of low humidity and warmth (48 hours before)
- Apply liquid manures (48 hours before)
- Fungus control - Spray with Equisetum tincture and spray with 501 early morning.
- Insect control -watch out for chewing and sucking insects.
- Look at using a Garlic/Ginger/Chilli pepper spray, natural pyrethrum, stinging nettle liquid mixed with 5% cow urine, neem oil or thuricide.
- Surround plants with diatomaceous earth (available from swimming pool suppliers).
- Drench animals for internal parasites 48 hours before full Moon on an empty stomach with garlic and cider vinegar.

ACTIVITIES CONNECTED WITH THE NEW MOON

- Avoid sowing seeds
- Avoid felling trees for timber
- Traditional Indian agriculture calls the day before a new Moon as 'no Moon day', a day on which no agricultural work is done.

MOON AND SATURN IN OPPOSITION
Occurs every 27.5 days

This is when the Moon and Saturn are positioned on opposite sides of the earth and their forces are raying in to the earth

from each direction. The Moon forces bring calcium processes which are connected to propagation and growth forms, while the Saturn forces bring silica processes which are connected to building up substance of the plant in root, leaf and fruit. The balancing effect of these two influences streaming into the earth produce very strong plants from seed sown at this time. It has been found that spraying with Preparation 501 at this time strengthens the plant to the extent that it can resist plant diseases and certain insect attacks. It can also increase nutritional quality, taste and shelf life after harvest.

ACTIVITIES CONNECTED WITH MOON OPPOSITE SATURN.

- Seed sowing and transplanting
- Spray with 501 at sunrise on the day or the day before the Moon opposes Saturn for fungus. For example, mildew and botrytis on grapes, rust on oats, mildew on tamarillos, blight on tomatoes and potatoes, greasy spot on passion fruit and mildew on curcubits. Please note that 501 is not a fungicide, rather it strengthens the plant to help it overcome the fungus.
- Preparation 501 used at this time improves the quality, taste and shelf life of all fruits and vegetables after harvest

Spraying 501 in early morning, Moon opposite Saturn.

MOON IN ZODIAC CONSTELLATIONS
Occurs every 27.3 days

The zodiac is a belt of fixed stars which are in groupings we call constellations. This belt ranges behind the ecliptic path of the Sun. All the planets including the Moon move in front of the zodiac constellations.

The Moon passes in front of the complete circle of the constellations every 27.3 days. Because the constellations are of different sizes, the Moon moves in front of each between one and a half and three and a half days. As the Moon passes in front of the different constellations it will focus certain favourable conditions to the plants. The zodiac constellations bring an emphasis of the four elements. The constellations and the element they represent are as follows:

- EARTH ELEMENT
  Root development
  Moon in front of Virgo – Capricorn – Taurus

- WATER ELEMENT
  Leaf development
  Moon in Cancer – Scorpio – Pisces

- AIR AND LIGHT ELEMENT
  Flower development
  Moon in Gemini – Libra – Aquarius

- WARMTH ELEMENT
  Seed Development and Fruit Development
  Moon in Leo – Sagittarius – Aries

The times of Moon passing through the Zodiac are given in annual planting calendars produced by biodynamic associations around the world. The influences of the particular constellations are brought into the soil through cultivation at the appropriate time, particularly where the soil is fertile and alive through biodynamic management. Germinating seeds also receive these influences, so if it is desired to promote certain influences, one sows the seed and cultivates during the favourable constellation period. These influences can also be brought to the plant by spraying 501 at the appropriate time.

ASCENDING AND DESCENDING OF THE MOON
Occurs every 27.3 days.

The Moon's daily path across the sky as seen from the earth is not always the same. Sometimes it is higher in the sky, sometimes lower, similar to the sun during its yearly cycle from summer to winter; the Moon goes through this cycle each month.

The Sun passes in front of the twelve zodiac constellations during the course of a year, from Gemini to Sagittarius, (mid winter to midsummer) which is ascending, and from Capricorn to Taurus, (midsummer to mid winter) which is descending.

The Moon moves in an arc from East to West and when these arcs get higher every day, the Moon is ascending and when they get lower every day the Moon is descending. The Moon takes 27.3 days to complete this cycle, each ascending and descending period lasting about two weeks. Please note that this is not the same rhythm as the new Moon – full Moon – new Moon rhythm which lasts 29.5 days.

The effects of the ascending and descending period can be compared to gestures presented by the seasons. An ascending period is much like the spring and summer of the year where the earth 'breaths out'. This is seen as an outpouring of growth activity above the soil surface where the life forces and saps flow upwards and fill the plant with vitality.

Although germination takes place below the ground, it also takes part in this upward striving. This is time to spray preparation 501.

The descending period on the other hand is related to the activity below the soil surface and can be compared with the autumn/winter time of year. The earth 'breathes in' and draws growth forces back down below the soil surface. Lower parts of the plant, especially the roots, are activated. This is the time for cultivation, composting and transplanting, also the time to apply preparation 500.

Tomatoes sown Moon opposite Saturn. Planted in pots during descending period.

ACTIVITIES CONNECTED WITH ASCENDING PERIOD

- Sow all seeds using the appropriate constellation and cultivate at the appropriate constellation before sowing.

For cereals	Warmth	Leo
For Fruits	Warmth	Sagittarius
For Leaf	Water	Cancer and Scorpio
For Flower	Air / Light	Gemini and Libra
For Roots	Earth	Virgo

- Spray with 501 at early stages of growth when the plant is recognisable and using appropriate constellation.
- Harvest on an Air / Light constellation:
    - Fruit and Vegetables (however not root vegetables)
    - Plants for making medicines
    - Flowers and plants for preparation making

ACTIVITIES CONNECTED WITH DESCENDING PERIOD

- Spray preparation 500 in autumn and early spring in the afternoon when the soil is warm
- Transplant seedlings and trees
- Make and spread compost
- Make and plant cuttings
- Cultivate soil at appropriate constellation time
- Harvest root crops for storage on an Earth day e.g. Taurus
- Prune all fruit trees in the appropriate season on fruit day e.g. Aries
- Prune flowering trees, shrubs and roses on a flowering day e.g. Aquarius

NODES
Occur approximately every 14 days

Moon node cycles occur at the point where the Moon's path crosses the path of the sun during ascending and descending. There is an ascending node and a descending node every month. This rhythm occurs every 27.2 days, so there is a node approximately every 14 days. The influence of the node lasts for around 6 hours either side. The Moon while crossing in front of the sun will negate the sun's beneficial influence for this brief period. This negative influence works into soil being freshly cultivated at the time of the node. Avoid any agricultural or horticultural work at the node. The effect is similar to that of an eclipse of the Sun by the Moon.

APOGEE AND PERIGEE
Occurs every 27.5 days

The Moon moves around the earth in an ellipse. The Moon's nearest point to the earth on the ellipse is called Perigee and the further most point is called Apogee.

At Apogee it appears to be a good time to plant potatoes as there seems to be a multiplicity of form (meaning more po-tatoes) where as at Perigee fewer potatoes are produced, but grow bigger.

At Perigee, when the Moon is closest, there is greater mois-ture and a tendency towards fungus growth. Look out for a perigee at full Moon as both bring moisture to the earth and thus the tendency to fungus is very strong. Use preparation 501. Apogee and Perigee times bring a stress period and seed sowing should be avoided 12 hours on either side of these times (except the planting of potatoes at Apogee).

ACTIVITIES CONNECTED TO MOON RHYTHMS

- 500 APPLICATION
  - During a descending period
  - In the afternoon
  - In the spring or in autumn

- 501 APPLICATION
  - During an ascending period at the beginning of the plant's growth, and later just before harvest or close to when the Moon is in opposition to Saturn. This will bring quality, taste and a longer shelf life. It will also strengthen the plant against fungus.

- SEED SOWING
  The following times have been found to be beneficial:
  - Moon opposite Saturn
  - Full Moon 48 hours before
  - During an ascending period (avoiding node, apogee, perigee and the new Moon)
  - Sow at the following times for the particular constellation effect on the ascending period:

Air Light	Flower	Gemini and Libra
Water	Leaf	Cancer and Scorpio
Warmth	Fruits	Sagittarius
Warmth	Seeds	Leo
Earth	Roots	Virgo

- TRANSPLANTING
  Seedlings, container grown plants, trees and shrubs at the descending period at the appropriate season

- COMPOST MAKING
  Best during descending period.

- COMPOST SPREADING
  Spread during descending period in autumn or early spring, depending on soil conditions and crop requirements.

- CULTIVATION & SOIL PREPARATION
  Best during the descending period. Where weather and soil conditions permit. Please note that cultivation of the soil when it is wet can cause structural damage.

- HARVESTING
  We have found that all crops keep better and main-

tain quality in storage if harvested during the air/ light period on the ascending Moon (like Gemini or Aquarius).

Avoid harvesting at full Moon, perigee and on leaf days (Cancer and Scorpio) - these are times of more water in the earth so crops would hold too much water for satisfactory storage. If seeds are to be saved, or grains harvested, choose a period when the Moon is in Leo. Roots and Potatoes should be harvested in a descending period when the Moon is in an earth constellation like Taurus.

- LIQUID MANURE APPLICATION
   The best time is just before full Moon in the afternoon. Liquid manures can be used several times during the growth of the crop.

- POTATO PLANTING
   Best done at Apogee. Usually at this time there are good numbers of medium size potatoes produced. Also there is often a resistance to the potato tuber moth.

- FULL MOON AND PERIGEE
   These are stress times and because of this they bring a watery influence to the earth and can lead to fungus attacks, especially during warmer weather from spring to autumn. Spray with Equisetum on days prior to and during these times. Spray with 501 in the early morning when the Moon is opposite Saturn, which will strengthen the plant to resist fungus.

- PRUNING
   Prune all fruit trees and berry shrubs on the descending Moon in the appropriate season. If possible choose a warm constellation time like Aries which

will encourage fruit bud formation. Prune all flowering shrubs and roses in the appropriate season at the descending Moon. If possible choose an air/light day e.g. Aquarius.

OTHER ASTRONOMICAL RHYTHMS WHICH APPEAR ON THE PLANTING CALENDAR

- SUN

   Knowing the sun's position in the zodiac is important for the peppering of insects.

- OTHER ASPECTS

   This shows the positions of the planets (including the Moon) in relationship to one another. These can be useful in endeavouring to determine and studying weather patterns. It is useful to make notes of each day's weather and check with the various planets position in the constellations.

   In the New Zealand Biodynamic calendar there is no adjustment made for daylight savings time.

- PEPPERING

   Guidelines are provided for those interested in using the methods of peppering to reduce the incidence of weeds, insects and rodents as indicated by Rudolf Steiner.

- WEEDS

   Seeds of nuisance weeds which are ripe and viable should be burnt at Full Moon or when the Moon is in Leo. The seeds are put in a small tin and placed in very hot fire. The resultant ash is mixed with fine sand or wood ash and spread over the land or potentised to a D6 or D8 and should be spread at Full Moon, and perhaps several times in the year. This also applies to burning runners of the roots of weeds like couch grass or the bindweed (morning glory) and then spreading the ash over the affected area. Please note that the potentizing can be done by a homeopath. It is also important to remember that some weeds are beneficial and are accumulators of trace elements. These should not be peppered but made into liquid manure.

• INSECTS

Insects are burnt in a similar way to weeds but here they are burnt at the time when the sun is in various Zodiac constellations. The effect ranges from when the sun is in Aquarius to when the Sun is in Cancer.

You will need to know the life cycle of the insect you are trying to deter, and then determine in which environment it spends the majority of time. E.g. the grass grub spends most of its life in the earth, so one would choose an earth constellation, like Taurus. The common house fly or mosquito spends most of its life in a watery environment in the larva stage, so one would choose a water constellation, like Pisces or Cancer.

If there are no insects around at the time for burning you will need to save some from where they are prevalent. Here are a few examples:

• Sun in Taurus is best for all hard shelled insects
• Sun in Gemini is best for fruit moths or ants
• Sun in Cancer is best for snails and slugs, mosquitoes and flies.

Maria Thun has added the refinement of using the Moon in the constellation as well as the Sun for burning the insect. For instance, if one is to burn a hard shelled insect, choose when both the Sun and the moon are in Taurus. The resultant ash can be potentised to D6 or D8 or the ash can be mixed with milk sugar or wood ashes and spread. The insect pepper should be applied regularly throughout the season.

- RODENTS

    Rudolf Steiner suggests burning the skin of rodents when Venus is in conjunction with Scorpio. This occurs in a period of three weeks any time from between mid October and first week in January. The burnt skin can be ground up and mixed with ash, or milk sugar and sprinkled lightly over the infected areas, or the ash can be potentised to D6 or D8 and can also be sprinkled over.

Roses and vegetables

CHAPTER 5

MAKING A COMPOST HEAP

An average sized home garden on a ¼ acre section would require between 3 and 4 cubic metres of finished compost per year for vegetables, flowers and fruits. That would be one heap 4 metres long 1.5 m wide and 1 metre high.

It is easiest to make four heaps during the year, each 2 metres long, 1 metre wide and 1 metre high, which will each yield approximately one metre of finished compost. This means a heap being made every two months during summer and autumn, which is the time when there is plenty of waste crop materials available. Making good compost can be greatly helped by sourcing any non-chemically contaminated animal manure, like cow or sheep dung which bring in nitrogen to feed the bacteria which break down the organic materials. If there is no animal dung available you can use the nitrogen fertilizer Blood and Bone. You will also need half a bale of organically or biodynamically grown straw or hay per small compost.

The heap is best built as a windrow and turned regularly, around every six weeks. This will aerate the heap and it also will give you a chance to check moisture content. The compost should be ready in about four months depending on the ambient temperature.

All composts require similar basic materials. There are two types of materials that are used in every heap. The protienaceous are materials which have high levels of protein which will form into organic nitrogen, like grass clippings or animal dung. Materials which contain a lot of carbon are known as carbonaceous, such as straw or dry autumn leaves. These are sometimes called wet (protein) and dry (carbon) and are used in the proportion of 60% protein and 40% carbon.

Some materials available in early summer:

PROTEIN
- Lawn clippings
- Weeds and fresh green grasses and leaves
- Legume green crops such as broad beans before flowering and blue lupines
- Shoots and young branches of legume trees such as tree lucern
- Kitchen scraps
- Animal dung

CARBON
- Crop wastes from late winter vegetable plants e.g. broad beans or other legume plants such as sweet pea vines or green pea plants
- Hedge cuttings and pruning
- Straw or Hay
- Shredded wood pruning

Some materials available in autumn:

PROTEIN
- Lawn clippings
- Weeds and green grasses and green leaves.
- Kitchen scraps
- Animal Dung

CARBON
- Autumn leaves
- Chopped up prunings from fruit trees
- Crop wastes from summer vegetable crops e.g. brassica stalks or pea or bean plants, sweet corn stalks
- Shredded wood chips
- Straw or hay

GREEN MATERIALS – AIR AND MOISTURE MAKE WARMTH

Attention must be given to the aeration of the compost heap. Without air, the heap won't heat up and it will become anaerobic and smelly. Firming the material down too much will exclude the air so try to keep the layers loose. Building an air tunnel at the bottom of the heap with layers of hay from a bale, or corn talks will stop the heap from settling down too much.

To have a successful fermentation, attention must be given to getting the right amount of protein plant or dung material, the right amount of moisture and the right air content. The temperature will then rise to about 60c.

Compost is best made in a layering technique. The carbonaceous layer should be about 10cm deep, alternating with the protein layer about 15cm deep. In this way the protein of the green will supply the nitrogen that bacteria require for their growth to break down the carbon material.

Care must be taken that the dry carbon material is moist enough. It is best to dampen down any dry material before it is put on to the heap. The dry material can be dipped into water in a barrow allowing excess water to drain off. Testing to

Lawn clippings & barley straw.

assess proper moisture content is achieved by checking that water can drip from the material when it is squeezed in the hand. The animal dung should be made into a slurry and watered onto the carbon layer. This will bring the animal effect into the compost and also feed the micro-organisms which will break down the dry material.

Apply hydrated lime to the green vegetation layer. You will need only a dusting, like sugar on porridge. Most soils need extra phosphate. This can be addressed by applying rock phosphate to the heap. Approx 5 kgs per one cubic metre sprinkled on the carbon layer. The compost should develop phosphate solubilizing bacteria which will gently work on the rock and make the phosphate available.

COMPOST SITE

It is best to make compost where there is shade. Such trees as Kowhai, Silver birch and Alder are beneficial to compost making and will provide valuable shade during the hot dry summer months. Avoid building heaps under trees with rampant roots eg. Willow or Pinus radiata as the roots will invade the compost.

Compost Yard – wheel barrow, kitchen scraps bin, grass & leaves, barrel of cow dung slurry, bale of straw.

MAKING A HOME COMPOST HEAP

1.   Mark out the size of the heap. In this case the heap will be 1.5 metres wide, 2 metres long and 1 metre high.

2.   Make an air tunnel using thin blocks of straw from the bale down the middle of the heap.

Tunnel of straw.

3.   Make a foundation bed of wet hay 10 cm deep over the proposed size of the heap. The straw is best wet before it is put onto the heap. Fill a barrow with water and use this to dunk the straw into Allow it to drain off and then put it on the heap. Any dry material is wet enough when water can be just squeezed out of it.

Wetting straw in barrow.

4.   Next sprinkle some slurry on the straw. Just lightly over.

Slurry on layer of straw.

5.   Put on a thick layer of green lawn clippings, about 15cm deep. This will begin to generate warmth through out the heap. Apply a sprinkle of hydrated lime over the green. The lime will hold the life force of the green material while it is breaking down.

Cow dung slurry & compost

6.   Put on a 10 cm layer of straw followed by more slurry. Follow with 15cm of green vegetable wastes - old runner and dwarf bean plants and any grasses or weeds. Place any weeds that are seeding in the middle of the heap with their roots to the outside so that their seeds will germinate and die within

the heat of the heap and thus help towards weed free compost. Apply a dusting of hydrated lime over the green. Then another layer of straw and another sprinkle of slurry. Apply a layer of kitchen scraps on the straw which have been accumulating in a covered bin since the last compost was made, perhaps two months ago.

These scraps have been sprinkled with Cow Pat Pit. Also add some dry leaves. The compost worms Eisena foedita are very active in these scraps.

Hydrated lime on lawn clippings.

Decomposing kitchen scraps can also have a light dusting of hydrated lime. Continue on with the layers in order:

- Green material either of lawn clippings or garden weeds long grass and chopped vegetable plants eg brassicas or hedge clippings sprinkled with hydrated lime.
- Dry material either straw or dry garden wastes i.e.chopped up sweet corn stalks.
- Runner bean vines or autumn leaves. Always use the slurry
- Any more kitchen scraps if we have them.
- When the desired height is reached finish off with a layer of old compost.

Add in the Biodynamic compost preparations 502 to 507. The preparations 502 to 506 are put separately into a small ball of compost. One gram of preparation for each ball. Then they are inserted into five holes along the side of the heap about 15 cm deep.

10mls of preparation 507 Valerian is mixed in 3 litres of rain water for 10 minutes (in alternating vortices) and one half of this is poured into two holes on the top of the heap with the remaining sprinkled over and around the heap. As cow pat pit is made using the compost preparations 502 – 507 it is possible to use cow pat pit liquid as an inoculant which is sprinkled on each layer of material while building the heap. Use 200 grams of CPP in 40 litres water stirred for 10 minutes and sprinkle approx 5 litres on each layer. If there is a known deficiency of phosphorous use rock phosphate on one of the layers of dry of the slurry. 10kg would be enough for a home garden for a period of three or four years.

Compost nearly completed.

The heap will start to heat up after two days. It can reach 60C and will gradually level out to about 40C after two weeks. When finished the heap can be covered with hessian sacks to keep in the warmth and to stop it drying out in hot weather. If heavy rain is imminent use a tarpaulin to keep out the rain. The heap should be turned after six weeks which will aerate it and also check if the material needs more water. The heap should smell nice with no Ammonia aroma. It should be ready to use in about four months.

A good rule while building the compost is to look after the edges and corners then the middle looks after itself. In this way we finish with a neat heap with no lumps or bumps where the heap could lose moisture.

If cow dung is not available to make slurry try to find some poultry manure from a free range organic poultry farm. Preferably collect the straw dung from the overnight shelters. Make this into slurry and apply it in the same way as with the cow dung slurry. If there is no animal manure available sprinkle blood and bone fertilizer on to the moist layer of

Preparations into old compost.

Putting preparations into finished compost pile.

straw as nourishment for the bacteria. Blood and bone has been heated to a high temperature during its manufacture and this treatment would break down many of the residuals that could be in it.

SUMMARY OF CHAPTER 5

- Compost is the best way to maintain Humus
- Good compost can be made using protein materials (such as lawn clippings and fresh green grasses and weeds and any animal dung) and carbonaceous materials (such as straw or hay, hedge cuttings and pruning's, dry crop wastes, shredded wood chips).
- For a good break down compost needs air, moisture and green material, which will make warmth.
- Start building the heap with an air tunnel with thin blocks of straw down the middle followed by layers of damp straw, cow dung slurry on the straw, thick layer of green lawn clippings with a sprinkling of Hydrated Lime, more damp straw, sprinkle cow dung slurry, 15cm of vegetable wastes, more damp straw or old vegetable wastes, slurry, lawn clippings. Add preparations 502 to 507.
- Turn heap after 6 weeks and again in another 6 weeks. Check moisture
- Site is important. Avoid trees with hungry roots and build in shady spot.
- Mature compost forked into soil before sowing or planting.

Layer of compost scraps – compost worms.

CHAPTER 6

MAKING A COW PAT PIT

If Cow manure is in plentiful supply it is a good idea to make a cow pat pit (CPP). This is cow manure which has been mixed with crushed egg shell and basalt dust and put into a 90cm x 60 cm pit, 30cm deep and lined with bricks. Cow Pat Pit the dung should only be one brick deep. It is fermented using one portion each of the preparations 502 – 506 which are put into small holes on the surface of the dung and a portion of 507 which is mixed in 5 litres of water and sprinkled over the surface of the dung. The pit is covered with a hessian sack and the dung is allowed to ferment as a type of specialized compost. It should be protected from the hot sun and heavy rain using a tarpaulin for shelter.

The process takes 4 to 6 months to break down, depending on the temperature. When ready it should be well decomposed with a soft fine structure. When mature it is mixed with water at the rate of 200grams per 1/4acre, in 40 litres of water stirred for 10 minutes. It is very used:

- As a foliar feed each month
- To inoculate compost with the preparations. Sprinkle two buckets of the CPP water on each layer while building
- Applied to tree bark to stimulate the cambium growth
- As a spray over roses and fruit trees to help heal pruning cuts
- As a seed bath
- For Soaking cuttings to enhance root development
- For dipping Seed potatoes for 5 minutes before planting to help control late blight.
- Stirred with cowhorn dung preparation 500, also to spray on the land to get the influences of the compost preparations 502 – 507 over the land. Use 25grams of 500 and 100grams CPP in 13 litres of water per acre. Stir for 1

hour as previously described
- With biodynamic cow horn silica preparation 501 as part of the sequential application of the biodynamic sprays.

The general rate of use is to mix 200 grams (about two heaped handfuls) in 40 litres of rain water for ¼ acre. It should be stirred for 15 minutes in a similar way that preparation 500 is stirred. Strain the liquid through a muslin cloth and spray it over the plants and the surrounding soil or sprinkle it over the land.

The idea of fermenting cow dung in such a way came from Maria Thun in Dexbach in northern Germany. She is well known in Biodynamic circles for her work with the planting calendar. She made the first fermented cow dung with the biodynamic compost preps in a barrel and it was known as barrel compost. You can often buy your cow pat pit from your local Biodynamic Association.

SUMMARY OF CHAPTER 6

The Cow Pat Pit is a very good way to bring strong biodynamic activity into your garden. Because it contains many plant growth hormones and a wide range of beneficial bacteria and fungi it can be used in many garden activities.

Cow Pat Pit showing brick construction – note the bottom of pit is bare earth.

CHAPTER 7

MAKING A LIQUID MANURE

A 50 litre food grade plastic drum or bucket will be big enough for a ¼ acre home garden for any of the liquid manures. Do not use a steel drum as these will rust and the rust in the water would affect the fermentation.

A large number of different liquid manures can be made in the garden from locally available plant materials, cow dung or seaweed which is fermented with preparations 502 – 507. Generally the liquid manures take from 8 to 12 weeks to be ready, depending on the temperature, the warmer the weather the faster the ferment. In all cases use the preparations Yarrow 502, Chamomile 503, Nettle 504, Oak bark 505, Dandelion 506 and Valerian 507.

When inserting the preparations into the liquid, make little "boats" out of a large leaf or half rotted straw. Fold the preparations up inside these and tie them up with a cotton thread and float these little "boats" with a preparation in each one on the surface of the liquid. They should float just slightly below the surface of the liquid. The forces of these herbal preparations will penetrate through the liquid. Then 10mls of Valerian 507 is stirred (in alternating vortices) in one litre of rain water for 10 minutes and poured into the liquid.

Cover the barrel with a hessian sack to stop evaporation and place in a warm shady area. After two weeks the liquid manure can be stirred for one minute every day or every second day. The stirring will help aerate the water and assist the fermentation.

After 8 weeks it should have a sweet smell and be ready to use. Apply by diluting one litre of the manure with nine litres of water and use over the whole garden. Liquid manures are used as a plant tonic and can be sprayed or sprinkled over leaves and the ground. They can be applied fortnightly, and with tomatoes it can be used weekly. It is good to apply liquid manures two days before full Moon.

SEAWEED

Chopped kelp off the beach makes excellent seaweed liquid as it can supply a wide range of major and trace elements to garden plants. King Neptune's necklace does not break down easily and sea lettuce has very little substance. Which seaweed you use will depend on availability. Bull kelp is also a great variety to use if you can get it.
The kelp can be dried and cut it up quite fine or it can be cut up while still wet. Fill one third to one half of a drum or bucket with this seaweed and then fill the drum almost to the top with rain water. Do not use water that is chlorinated or has had fluoride added. Otherwise use a locally made seaweed meal (not imported). In the case of seaweed powder add 4kg of to 50 litres of water, making the powder into a paste before filling the drum or bucket up.

LIQUID COW MANURE

Make this wonderful tonic by using one third of a drum of cow dung to a full drum of water, and adding the preparations as above. Usual rate of application of all the liquid manures is one to ten that is one litre of liquid manure to nine litres of water per ¼ acre.

PLANT MATERIALS

Plants such as stinging nettles, lucern, casurina and various weeds are some of the options for liquid manures. The method is to fill the drum ¾ full with the plant material and cover with water. Add preparations and dilutions as above.

SUMMARY OF CHAPTER 7

- It is very easy to make the liquid brew. It can be used at fortnightly intervals as a foliar feed for vegetables and flowers for strong early growth and it can be used as a plant tonic.
- Made from such materials as cow dung, seaweed meal and plant materials like stinging nettle, lucern, green crops and various weeds.
- It is always made using the Biodynamic preparations and is a good way of bringing the influences of the biodynamic preparations to the plants and to the soil.

Liquid manure barrel

CHAPTER 8

GREEN MANURE
CROPPING

Green manures are fast growing legumes and or grasses, like blue lupin, vetch, rye corn or black oats, grown during the autumn and winter months. Digging them into the soil in spring is a great way to increase organic matter, resulting in increased humus in the soil. This plays a very important role in maintaining and improving soil fertility. Green manure can be dug into the soil within 12 to 16 weeks of sowing or, if land availability permits, it can be left for longer, but it should be dug in before flowering. Alternatively the plants can be grown on for a while and used for compost or liquid manure. After digging in, allow three weeks for the crop to break down before you sow your next crop. Applying a soil spray of cow pat pit will assist the breakdown. Green manure crops can also be grown in the spring after the winter vegetables have been harvested. They mature much quicker at this time of the year and will be ready to dig within 8 to 10 weeks.

It is a good idea to apply compost before sowing your green crop which will do two things:

1. Grow more bulk of material in your crop
2. Provide an active microbial life to assist the conversion of your green material into humus when it is dug in

Growing green crops prevents the leaching of soil nutrients in the wet winter months; it will also stimulate biological activity. If it is possible always apply preparation 500 and cow pat pit before sowing. This will encourage strong nitrogen root nodulation activity in legumes. Sow seeds at the Moon opposite Saturn to ensure good germination and strong growth. Green manures help to control insect pests and weeds and will prevent excess water runoff during wet periods. Green manures can be grown at the end of the growing season or in between crops. Remember to dig your green crop in before it flowers as the maximum leaf proteins are in the plant before the seeding process begins.

Some of the legume species which are suitable for quick growth:

Blue lupin	+	
Broad bean	+	#
Tic bean	+	#
Vetch	+	
Green peas		#
Dwarf beans		#

These can be sown with:

Oats	+	
Rye Corn	+	
Barley		#
Wheat		#
Buck wheat		#
Mustard		#
Phacelia		#
French Marigold		#

Nodules on Blue Lupins.

+   sow in Autumn
#   sow in Spring

Care needs be taken that crop rotation also applies to green cropping so as to avoid any build up of fungus diseases in legumes or club root in mustard, which is the same family as the cabbage and rocket. The home gardener can grow a green crop between the rows of trees which can be cut and used as mulch to drought proof the trees.

In the autumn or early spring, when there is space in your vegetable garden, sow a mixture of grains and legumes. The grains bring in carbonaceous and the legumes provide the protein element. Every district has species which do well. The above suggestions are suitable green crop species of legumes and grain suitable for temperate climates like New Zealand, Southern Australia and South Africa around Capetown.

In spring to enliven a piece of land which has grown winter vegetables sow a mixture of legumes and grains as above. These would be ready to dig in by early summer.

For tropical areas such as Queensland, Fiji, Sri Lanka, India, Hawaii some legume species that are suitable for quick growth:

- Horse Gram
- Velvet Beans
- Cow pea
- Sunhemp

Some grain species that are suitable for green crop

- Millet
- Sorghum

These can be dug into the soil within 6 weeks of sowing, or if land availability permits can be left for a longer time but should be dug in before flowering. Alternatively the growth can be used for compost or liquid manure.

Slower growing tree species like Sesbania can be grown as grown as an annual and can be grown together with Velvet bean. After 4 months will it produce a great bulk of biomass which can be composted or made into liquid manure or dug into the soil. After harvest the orchardist can scarify between the rows of trees and sow a green crop under mangos, guavas or bananas. Try for instance sunhemp, cowpea or cluster bean.

The orchardist can grow a green crop between the rows of trees which can be cut and used as a mulch to help drought proof trees.

CHAPTER 9

VEGETABLE GROWING

One of the most wonderful things about a home garden is growing your own vegetables. Success in growing vegetables can be as simple as knowing which variety to plant and when to do so. This means knowing the variety of vegetable for the season and what time of the year to sow. For continuity of supply research will be needed into sowing and planting times.

For long term crops, such as leeks, you will need to be thinking up to nine months. With a short term crop (in New Zealand) seeds are sown in September, planted out in December and harvested in May to September. On the other hand, short term salads such as radish and rocket are sown in September and are harvested continuously from the beginning of November on.

SOIL AND BED PREPARATION

After the bed is dug over, apply your biodynamic compost at the rate of one wheel barrow spread evenly over 6 square

Tomatoes, Dwarf Beans, Sweet Corn.

metres. Lightly fork in the compost, level and smooth off. All of the aforementioned soil preparations apply to the sowing and planting of vegetables.

- Plan a crop rotational bed scheme. See table at end of chapter
- Avoid working wet soils
- Avoid treading on or compacting wet soils
- Use a plank to put on the ground to tread on while sowing or planting.
- Apply compost at the descending period of the Moon
- Prepare soil for sowing or planting at the descending of the Moon
- Cultivate vegetables at the descending period of the Moon and according to the relevant zodiac constellation

SOWING SEEDS - IN THE OPEN GROUND.

The tilth of the soil is very important for successful seed sowing. The finer the seed the finer the tilth should be.
Level off the soil using a rake; next make a shallow furrow approximately the depth of the seed. For smaller seeds like radish, rocket, carrot, parsnips, or silver beet make a furrow 2.5 cm deep using the end of the rake handle. Carefully cover the seeds and firm down with the back of the rake. For seeds like peas, beans or sweet corn make a furrow using the side of a rake about 5cm deep. Peas and beans can be sown in a double row. With broad beans, which are quite a big seed, the furrow can be up to 7.5 cm deep.

When sown in the furrow the seeds can be carefully covered over with soil making sure you do not cover them too deep. Lightly firm the soil with the back of the rake. Mark the rows with stakes and label with variety date and constellation.
Most vegetables can be grown in rows between 30 and 45 cm apart depending on the size of the plant. Sweet corn, a

tall grower, should be 90 cm apart between rows and plants.
Runner beans are easily grown up a bamboo tripod. Seeds
are sown 30cm apart
Pumpkin, squash, cucumber and similar are grown on mounds
or hills 90 cm apart. Additional compost is incorporated into
the mounds which are smoothed off and firmed with the
back of the rake. The seeds are pressed into the mound about
1 to 2.5 cm deep.

SOWING, DEPTH, AND INTER-ROW DISTANCES

Plant	Depth	Distance between rows
Radish	2.5cm	20cm
Rocket	2.5 cm	20 cm
Carrot	2.5 cm	25 cm
Parsnip	2.5cm	30 cm
Red Beet	2.5 cm	30 cm
Silver Beet	2.5 cm	35 cm
Peas	5 cm	30 cm
Dwarf Beans	5 cm	35 cm
Runner Beans	5cm	35cm between clumps
Broad Beans	7.5 cm	40 cm
Sweet Corn	5 cm	80 cm and plants
Pumpkin, Squash, Cucumber	2.5 cm	On mounds 80cm apart, 3 plants per mound

A FEW NOTES WHEN SOWING SEEDS IN BOXES OR TRAYS.

• Small plastic seedling trays are ideal for starting seeds of
lettuce cabbage, cauliflower, broccoli, peppers and tomatoes.

- Use moist sieved mature compost. Level the soil in a tray with a block of wood and firm down about 2.5cm from the top.
- Sprinkle seed lightly over surface of soil in tray and press lightly into the soil. Cover with the lightest amount of the sieved compost and lightly press this soil down.
- Put the tray into a white plastic bag and fold down the opening. This will maintain the moisture level during germination and stop the soil in the tray from drying out. The white plastic of the bag gives sufficient light to encourage germination.
- Put tray into a warm place, a small glass house if you have one, or on a sunny veranda or window ledge.
- Check moisture content of the soil every other day and lightly moisten if necessary
- After 5 to 7 days germination has begun. Allow more air into the bag each day and after another 7 days take the tray out of the bag.
- The young seedlings will harden off on the veranda, and after another 5 to 7 days they can be transplanted (called 'pricking out') into seedling trays of more sieved moist mature compost. Make sure you get soil around the young seedling's roots. Firm plants in the mix using two fingers.
- If possible choose a descending period of the Moon for the pricking out.
- Lightly water with watering can rose. Put back on the warm veranda. Check the water daily.
- Plants will be ready to transfer into the garden about 4 weeks from pricking out, and they should be hardened off before planting. This means taking the tray off the warm veranda or out of the glasshouse and putting it in the place where they will be planted out. Harden off for three to four days.
- Tomato, pepper and aubergine can be started off germinating in the hot water cupboard. They need warm soil to germinate. As soon as germination has begun

put them in the glass house or on the warm veranda and gradually open up the plastic bag as they begin to grow and then remove the bag. They will be ready to prick out in 14 days approx after sowing.

GETTING THE GROUND READY FOR TRANSPLANTING SEEDLINGS

Prepare your land in much the same way as you prepare you soil for seed sowing with compost. Mark out planting rows on the bed. Allow between 30cm and 45cm between rows and 30cm between plants.

Take your well grown plants out of the tray and break off each plant with its roots like a piece of cake and place them on the marked out soil. Dig a hole with a trowel and firm the plant in. Water the plants right after they are planted, and it is a good idea to put a small amount of cow pat pit in the water to assist new root development.

It is best to do the transplanting in the afternoon to allow the re-establishment of the roots during the evening. Always do your planting during a descending period of the Moon. There is a rapid re-establishment of new roots at this time.

TOMATOES

Plant tomatoes 100cm apart. Make a hole and put one shovel full of fresh compost. Cover up the hole and plant. Put the stake in at the same time. As the plant grows keep well tied and prune out the laterals. Frequent sprayings with cow pat pit and liquid seaweed will help strengthen the plant against fungus attack.

AUBERGINES AND CAPSICUM

These grow in similar conditions to tomatoes but are perhaps more sensitive to the cold. Plant out about 40cm apart. Use cow pat pit and liquid seaweed.

ONIONS - RED OR WHITE

These can be sown in the open ground in late autumn or sown in seedling boxes in late winter. Plant out in early spring about 15cm apart. The red variety will be ready first.

Onions ready to harvest, cabbage ready to pick, potatoes need staking, yarrow & chamomile in background.

Stored onions.

POTATO

Greened up potatoes are best for planting. This can be achieved by putting them outside under a tree and away from frost, where they are in sunlight. A week before planting cut up any big tubers allowing 3 good eyes to develop. The cut surface will dry before planting. On the day of planting dip the tubers into a solution of cow pat pit for a few minutes, this will help with root development and help the potato to grow strongly without getting blight. The soil should be prepared as previously described. Make a trench 30cm deep and plant the tubers in the bottom of the trench 30cm apart. Cover in the trench.

When the first shoots appear and have grown 15cm high do the first moulding up by lightly covering over those shoots. As the shoots go on growing continue the moulding up until the ridges reach about 30cm high. You can make two plantings. It has been found that planting potatoes when the Moon is in apogee, which is when it is most distant from the earth, brings very good results.

HERBS

Herbs are easy to grow in most home gardens. They will do well in your soil of compost and biodynamic preparations. Herbs are either sown annually or they are perennial and therefore are not sown each year. Sow annual seeds in early spring at Moon opposite Saturn. Perennials are propagated in the autumn either by division of roots or by taking cuttings.

SUMMARY OF CHAPTER 9

* Soil and Bed Preparation. Make sure that your ground is well prepared with green manure, mature compost, application of good Biodynamic compost.
* Apply preparation 500 and the cow pat pit.

- Compost is well forked in and the beds are raked level and there is a good tilth to the soil
- Success in growing vegetables is knowing which variety of vegetable to sow or plant and when.
- Sowing seed in trays and planting out seedlings. The more you practise this the more skilful you will become.

Mulching Fejoa with compost & straw.

CHAPTER 10

FRUITS SUITABLE FOR THE HOME GARDEN

The soil around your fruit trees and bushes should receive the full range of preparations in the course of applying the preparations over the rest of the garden. It is recommended to apply cow horn dung preparation 500 plus the cow pat pit four times a year, twice in spring and twice in autumn. Each of your various fruit trees and bushes should receive adequate Biodynamic compost around the root zone to a depth of about 3cm lightly fork this into the soil. On top of the compost put about 5cm of biodynamic straw to keep the moisture in the compost and the soil, the mulch will also serve to keep down the weeds.

Apply cow pat pit as a spray over the whole plant and around the root zone once a month. Apply Horn silica 501 as part of the sequential spray over the whole garden.

- APPLE
  Grown on a dwarf root stock EM9. One large apple tree can be planted where it can be a shade tree and whose long keeping and late maturing fruit can be preserved. Renet de Thorn is a great variety.

- APRICOTS
  Need warm dry conditions and freedom from late frosts at flowering time. Use cow pat pit and Equisetum 508 as for peaches and nectarines to control brown rot of the fruit.

- CITRUS
  These do best if the garden is frost free or they can be grown in a sheltered position. All the citrus are surface

feeders and benefit from a generous application of good quality compost around the root zone in early spring. It is a good idea to mulch with straw on top of the compost application to keep in the moisture.

- FEJOA
An excellent bush for a regular supply of fruits in autumn needs plenty of compost and mulch during early spring. Lightly prune in autumn after fruiting. Benefits from regular cow pat pit sprays once a month.

- PEACHES AND NECTARINES
These trees also grow large but can be quite ornamental in the home garden. Generally they are prone to leaf curl and brown rot. Choose a variety that is resistant to these two diseases. Using a tree paste of cow pat pit and Equisetum 508 on the bark at bud movement in can help and also a bud spray of the same in mid August and thereafter at 14 day intervals until leaves are fully out. Preparation 501 at Moon opposition to Saturn will help to control curly leaf and the brown rot.

- PEARS
A great fruit which does well but the trees do get very big. They can be judiciously pruned.

- PLUMS
Good for home garden but do spread to be a large tree. Black Doris is a reliable jam making variety.

- PASSION FRUIT
Can be grown where you have a spot that gets full morning sun until midday. Plants need plenty of space to climb on a sunny wall or fence. They will crop in their second year and should be lightly pruned after flowering. They

like plenty of compost with mulch and regular spraying of cow pat pit.

- ## BLACKBERRY AND BOYSENBERRY
  Can be grown on a sunny fence. The canes which bore fruit last season should be cut out and the new season's canes tied down on the fence. Apply compost around root zone and mulch with straw.

- ## GOOSEBERRIES AND BLACKCURRANTS
  Best in cooler districts where fruiting wood is ripened by winter frosts. Fruits on old wood. Prune to keep bush open with the objective of ease of picking. Apply compost, cow pat pit and mulch in early spring.

- ## GRAPES
  Grown on a sunny fence if you have the space. In winter prune back laterals to the main stem leaving two buds on the laterals from which the flowers and then the fruit will come.

- ## RASPBERRIES
  These do very well in most temperate gardens. Prune out all last season's fruit bearing canes as they fruit on last season's new growth. The secret is to apply heavy dressings of biodynamic compost in spring and early autumn and keep them moist. Regularly apply cow pat pit and preparation 501 at Moon opposition to Saturn. They will need protection from the birds.

- ## STRAWBERRIES.
  These are grown and treated as annuals and grow well in a sunny position. Young plants are planted out in late autumn into a well composted area on ridges with 45 cm between ridges. Plant about 30cm apart. Mulch in early

spring with straw to keep the moisture in the ground and to also help with weed control. During the growing season keep the runners well cut back.

SUMMARY OF CHAPTER 10

- A description of which fruits are easy to grow.
- Yearly composting and mulching in late winter and early spring.
- Regular applications of the biodynamic preparation 500 twice in spring and twice in autumn.
- Apply the Cow Pat Pit over the whole plant and around the root zone once a month.
- Apply the horn silica as part of the sequential spray over the whole garden. See sequential spray chapter 3.

CHAPTER 11

ROSE GROWING

Roses like to be fed. They love well matured compost best given twice a year; once after pruning in late winter and again after the first flush of flowers are finished in summer. The summer application can be followed by a mulch of straw which will help maintain the moisture level in the soil during the hot summer. Spray regularly with cow pat pit, especially after pruning which will help seal the cuts and initiate new bud development.

Pruning is best done in late winter when the danger of frost has past. Everybody has their own ideas on pruning, but basically it is to keep the stems of the plant from getting too old so any growth older than three years should be cut out. Always try to prune to a bud pointing outwards from the centre which encourages an open growth in the centre. It seems like the best flowers grow on last year's growth.

Try to prune on a descending period of the Moon during a flower constellation. Aquarius is the flower constellation in

the southern hemisphere, and Gemini and Libra in the northern hemisphere. Summer pruning is a continuous job of cutting back the finished flowers. Prune back to a strong bud and you will have a new flower in no time.

Climbing roses take more time to prune. The overall method is the same, cutting out any wood over three years old. Encourage new growth and tie down last years growth from which you will get a mass of flowers. Climbers will need an extra bit of feeding.

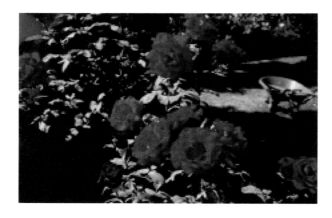

CHOOSING VARIETIES TO PLANT

I like to grow a rose that has a history of growing successfully in the district, one which grows and flowers well and does not have disease problems.

PLANTING A ROSE

Prepare the hole well. Incorporate plenty of well matured compost. Make sure the roots are well developed when selecting the new bush. Firm the soil well around the roots. Select three healthy shoots and prune back to three buds.
Disease and pest control does not seem to be a problem where good biodynamic practices are carried out especially if you choose a strong growing rose. The main diseases are black spot, leaf rust and mildew. I have found that most roses growing in a live biodynamic soil gain strength and can overcome these diseases. Regular cow pat pit goes a long way to strengthen health, as does spraying with 501 at the Moon opposite Saturn time.

MORE ON FLOWERS

Satisfying flower growing is like successful vegetable growing. It depends on soil quality, use of the biodynamic preparations, choosing the appropriate sowing and planting times and growing the right variety in the right season.   Everything we have discussed under vegetable growing applies equally well to flower growing. Compost, Compost, Compost.

CHAPTER 12

DISEASES AND PEST CONTROL

In a well run biodynamic garden with very good soil there should be little problem with pests and diseases. A plant is usually attacked if it is weak or under stress. Nature tries to eliminate the poorly growing plant. To grow strong annual vegetables and flowers try the following:

- Grow plants that do well in your district
- Choose healthy seed from strong plants in your garden or from biodynamic or organic gardens.
- Sow and grow in the correct season.
- Grow in soil that has had preparation 500, cow pat pit and biodynamic compost regularly applied and where a green crop has been grown regularly.
- Sow seeds at the time of Moon opposition to Saturn.
- In times of high humidity where mildew or other fungus could be a problem apply preparation 508 equisetum on the soil around the plant especially coming up to full Moon, or spray biodynamic 501 silica in the morning at Moon opposite Saturn.
- Biodynamic Silica 501 sprayed at Moon opposite Saturn strengthens the plant against fungus and insects.

CABBAGE, ROSES, APPLES AND PEACHES

For chewing insects, for instance the Cabbage White Butterfly which can decimate many of the cabbage family, one can use a bio control agent called Thuricide which contains Bacillus thurginensis and is very effective against the Cabbage White and other chewers. For all aphids use stinging nettle

(Urtica dioica) soaked in water for 24 hours and sprayed on the plant using soft soap as a spreader. The formic acid in the nettle sting goes into the water and irritates the soft body of the aphis. Do this for three evenings in a row.

Nettle can be used for all sucking insects. Nettle liquid manure can also be made with biodynamic preparations and adding 5% cow urine. Strain and make up 1/5 and spray.

Other recipes for sprays against chewing insects and sucking insects in the home garden:

Garlic	100g	soaked in vegetable oil over night
Chilli powder	100g	boiled in water
Ginger	100g	boiled in water
Soap	50g	made into liquid

Make up to 10 litres and spray

Ginger powder	100g	make paste
Turmeric powder	100g	make paste

Make up to 10 litres and spray

- Boil leaves and seeds of Melia (Indian Bead Tree) the, strain and spray
- Liquid tea of African marigold – Fill a container with the flowers, cover with rainwater, soak flowers for 7 days and spray
- Bacillus Thuringensis – Spray for codlin moth in apples and the cabbage white butterfly caterpillar
- Pheremone traps during flowering are effective in disrupting the mating of the codlin moth and if this proves

unsuccessful try a follow up spray with Thuricide.
- Encourage predator wasps by planting wild flowers.
- Autumn sown green crops will strengthen the soil and discourage insects over winter in the soil.

FUNGUS

Equisetum 508 100g of herb boiled for 20 minutes. Leave for 48hrs and strain. Make up to 10 litres and apply to the ground early in the season at each Perigee and full Moon before the fungus appears. Also use preparation 501 Silica applied early in the morning at Moon opposition to Saturn.

CHAPTER 13

LAWNS

A well mown lawn which is green and fresh will enhance the home garden. Use a strong grass seed mixture that will stand up to wear and tear and will provide regular contribution to the compost heap and food for bees.

Encourage the growth of perennial rye, white clover and fescue. This mix will withstand dry weather. Local grasses and weeds will also establish themselves and will all contribute to the greenness of the lawn and the compost making. Regular application of the 500 will also help keep the lawns green.

APPENDIX

SUGGESTED CROP ROTATION FOR A HOME GARDEN

Bed	Year 1			Year 2			Year 3		Year 4
	Autumn	Spring	Autumn	Spring	Autumn	Spring	Autumn
1	Winter Veg	Roots	WGC	Beans & Peas	WGC	Cabbage Salad	WGC
2	Winter Veg	SGC	Winter Veg	Roots	WGC	Beans & Peas	WGC
3	Winter Veg	SGC	Winter Veg	SGC	Winter Veg	Roots	WGC
4	WGC	SGC	Winter Veg	SGC	Winter Veg	SGC	Winter Veg
5	WGC	Cabbage Salad	WGC	SGC	Winter Veg	SGC	Winter Veg
6	WGC	Beans & Peas	WGC	Cabbage Salad	WGC	SGC	Winter Veg

WGC = Winter green crop: rye corn or oats together with vetch, blue lupind, tick beans.
SGC = Summer green crop: barley, wheat, oats or buckwheat together with vetch, broad beans, French beans.

HOME GARDENER'S SEED-GROWING AND PLANTING GUIDE FOR VEGETABLE GROWING IN THE SOUTHERN HEMISPHERE.

MONTH	SOW	PLANT	HARVEST
July	Broccoli Fordhook	Aug/Sept	Nov/Dec
(under glass)	Cabbage Golden Acre	Aug/Sept	Nov/Dec
	Derby Day	Aug/Sept	Nov
	Cauli All year round	Aug/Sept	Nov/Dec
	Four-Month Phenomenal	Aug/Sept	Nov/Dec
	Lettuce Triumph	Aug/Sept	Nov

MONTH	SOW	PLANT	HARVEST
August	Broccoli Fordhook	Sept/Oct	Dec/Jan
(under glass)	Cabbage Golden Acre	Sept/Oct	Dec/Jan
	Derby Day	Sept/Oct	Dec/Jan
	Cauli All year round	Sept/Oct	Dec/Jan
	Four-Month Phenom-enal	Sept/Oct	Dec/Jan
	Lettuce Great Lakes	Sept	Nov/Dec
	Buttercrunch	Sept	Nov/Dec

MONTH	SOW	PLANT	HARVEST
September	Cabbage Succession	Nov	Jan/Feb
(under glass)	Green Acre	Nov	Jan/Feb
	Lettuce Great Lakes	Oct	Dec
	Buttercrunch	Oct	Dec
	Oak Leaf	Oct	Dec
	Tomato Hardicross	Oct/Nov	Jan/Mar
	(dwarf)		
	Moneymaker (tall)	Oct/Nov	Jan/Mar
	or own choice		
	Celery Utah	Nov	Feb/Mar
	Green Peppers Yoyo	Nov	Feb/Apr
(outdoors)	Leeks	Jan	Apr/Aug
	Onions Pukekohe		Dec/Feb
	(long keeper)		
	California Red		Dec/Feb
	Carrot Topweight		Dec
	Chantenay		Dec
	Manchester Table		Dec
	Parsnip Hollow Crown		May/Aug
	Spinach		Oct/Nov
	Silverbeet		Dec/Sept
	Red Beet		Nov/May

MONTH	SOW	PLANT	HARVEST
October	Celery Utah	Jan	May/Aug
(under glass)	Cabbage Savoy-type	Jan	May/Aug
(outdoors)	Brussels Sprouts	Jan	May/Aug
	Curly Kale	Jan	May/Aug
	Lettuce Great Lakes		Dec/Jan
	Buttercrunch		Dec/Jan
	Dwarf & Climbing Beans, Pumpkin,		
	Cucumber, Melons, Corn		Jan/Mar
	Carrot Topweight		Jan/Mar
	Chantenay		Jan/Mar
	Manchester Table		Jan/Mar
	Parsnip Hollow Crown		May/Aug
	Spinach		Nov/Dec
	Silverbeet		Dec/Sept
	Red Beet		Dec/Jan
November	Cabbage Savoy-type	Jan	Apr/July
(outdoors)	Curly Kale	Jan	May/July
	Lettuce Great Lakes		Jan/Feb
	courgettes, carrots, beetroot		Mar/July
December	Cabbage Winter Cross	Feb	May/June
(outdoors)	Cauli White Acre	Feb	May/June
	Broccoli Shogun	Feb	Apr/June
	Lettuce Great Lakes		Jan/Feb
	Buttercrunch		Jan/Feb
	Corn – last sowing		March
	Carrot		Apr/July

MONTH	SOW	PLANT	HARVEST
January	Cabbage Winter Cross	Mar	Jun/Aug
(outdoors)	Cauli White Acre	Mar	Jun/Aug
	Broccoli Shogun	Mar	Jun/Aug
	Lettuce Great Lakes type		Feb/Mar
	Buttercrunch		Feb/Mar
	Mignonette	Mar	Apr/May
	Cos	Mar	Apr/May
February	Cabbage Winter Cross	end Mar	Jul/Sept
(outdoors)	Cauli White Acre	end Mar	Jul/Sept
	Broccoli Shogun	end Mar	Jul/Sept
	Lettuce Mignonette	end Mar	Apr/May
	Cos	end Mar	Apr/May
	Spinach		Apr/May
March	Spinach		Apr/May
April	Broadbeans		Sept/Oct
	Spinach		Jun/July

ACKNOWLEDGEMENTS

I would like to thank Hamish MacKay of the Australian Bi-odynamic Association in Bellengen N.S.W. whose idea this booklet was and whose encouragement and advice made it happen and for the great support from my partner, Rachel Pomeroy, whose on-going work with our garden has been wonderful.

From Andy Black of Weleda in Hawkes Bay whose practical appraisement of the manuscript was very valuable, and lastly to Murray Childs at Copyplus Hastings and Thomas Proctor whose help in the layout and editing was great.

CPSIA information can be obtained
at www.ICGtesting.com
Printed in the USA
LVIC06n2202090214
373017LV00005B/10